POETIC STORIES
from THE EYES OF MY WINDOWS

BY ANGELLIA MOORE

October 9, 2010

ISBN: 978-1-4269-4734-6 (sc)
ISBN: 978-1-4269-4735-3 (e)

Trafford rev. 01/05/2011

 www.trafford.com

North America & international
toll-free: 1 888 232 4444 (USA & Canada)
phone: 250 383 6864 ♦ fax: 812 355 4082

To

My Mother

Family and Friends

This work is dedicated to my family who always held lively conversations about me as I sat around the house during the days of my youth reading books, drawing illustrations, listening to music, and writing stories, poems, and lyrics to songs on the radio.

Also, this book is dedicated to my many wonderful friends who have added lasting memories to my life in general. It was my family and host of friends who helped me celebrate life as I know it today. Thank you to each one of you for carving your own special place in my heart and in this work.

PREFACE

Certainly, I would like to thank God, His son, Jesus Christ, and the Holy Spirit for the all of the inspirations given to me to write this work. Many of the poetic stories in this work are based on memories of actual events and inspired thoughts. The Holy Spirit often brought back to my remembrances events, people, and details that were lying in dormant places in my memory over the years. Thank you, God.

TABLE OF CONTENTS

CHAPTER 3: Poetic Stories From the Eyes of my Consciousness

CHAPTER 4: Poetic Stories from the Eyes of my Family and Friends

Chapter 5: Poetic Stories from the Eyes of Love

INTRODUCTION

The poems in *Poetic Stories: from the Eyes of My Windows* are inspired writings from actual people around me, actual events in my life, and ideas in my head and heart. What I like about these poetic stories is that no two stories are alike. Each one tells its own story and takes on its own design and meaning. The inspiration for each one comes when it comes; therefore the poems are written at various times, and several of the poetic stories are from past experiences.

I tried to use various literary devices. So, as you read, you will see and hear varied rhyme scheme patterns. You will hear multiple usage of repetition, and you will hear examples of metaphors, similes, onomatopoeia, and certainly imagery.

All of the poetic stories are from the eyes of my window, the depths of my soul, from my mind's perspective, and from my inspirations. I was inspired and motivated to write each one for one reason or another to share with you as a reader. This work intends to give you an insight as to what I was thinking, feeling, and going through. It explains how each poem came about from a mere thought, a past experience, or an action. There are several poems that fall into the category as my favorites, and I hope several of these poems will become your favorite as well.

Readers, will you do me a favor? Read the poetic stories at random. Do not read the book from the first poem to the last one; go from poem to poem at random. I think you will certainly enjoy reading the poems that way. I did not write the poems in a chronological order. A few of them were written at various times and for various reasons. Many were written for the compilation of this work. Go to the Table of Contents, select a poem, read it, and go from there.

CHAPTER 1: Poetic Stories

from the Eyes of

Youthful Bliss

Summer Fun is a poem that I remember writing when I was in the eighth grade. I wrote it for my English class. That morning after arriving at school, one of my friends didn't have her homework. Well, she wanted to copy my poem, this poem. I didn't know any better at the time, so I let her copy my poem. Just so happened she went to the English class before me. She submitted my poem as her poem. When I got to the same class a few hours later, the teacher recognized that this poem had already been submitted. She questioned me. I told her I wrote the poem, and my friend copied it. I do not remember the consequence or the grade I received, but it never happened again, thanks to that teacher.

Summer Fun

Summer fun
is lying in the sun,
drinking a pop,
and playing hopscotch.

Summer fun
is playing in the sun,
lying under a shady tree,
and counting colorful things you see.

red lady bugs   orange butterflies   yellow sunshinea

green trees   pink flowers

yellow bumble bees

One day I was standing in my classroom while the students were engaged in a standardized test. I was prompting and monitoring my students as they worked. My mind wondered a little bit. I thought about how it takes a great teacher to bring the scattered minds of these students together, in one place, and on the same accord during a class period and a school day. Thus, the poetic story of *Scattered Minds* was created.

Scattered Minds

Going places

Running races

Scattered minds

    Bright eyes

    Crying smiles

    Scattered minds

        Talking loud

        Boisterous crowds

        Scattered minds

            Rapping songs

            Having fun

            Scattered minds

                Trying drugs

                Being thugs

                Scattered minds

                    Hiding guns

                    Life-on-the run

                    Scattered minds

                        Seeking peace

                        Dying on the street

                        Scattered minds

Heather was one of my students when she was in the fourth grade. That's at least fifteen years ago. I was in the early stages of my teaching career. Heather and her classmates were my pride and joy. I enjoyed working with those students so much. This story is about Heather and how she always anticipated my next move, next step, and need in the classroom. Although she did her work like the other students, she was attuned to me. I called her Little Heather because she was physically small for her age, and she was smaller than the other fourth grade students. Little Heather was energetic, lively, smart, and very aware. This is her story from the eyes of my windows.

Little Heather

Once I had a student
As charming as can be,
Always at my right hand,
Always assisting me.

She was really short
Even for a 4th grade kid
Sitting there in the front row
Crossed-legged like a little Indian kid.

Every move I made
Her eyes were right there
"Do you need help with that, Ms. Moore?
I can take it somewhere."

She watched me while she worked
From here to there around the room
She was there to assist
Her aid would come to me soon.

She knew what I needed
Before I could ever get it out
She had already volunteered
Before I could open my mouth.

Little Heather was always happy
With a smile on her face
One day, thick tears
took that smile's place.

I just talked with her
To make things right
Let her know things were okay
She will be alright.

For whatever reason, I was her idol
Little Heather's saving grace
Knowing that I cared
Put that smile back on her face.

I can't remember her work habits
I'm sure she was a good student
what I remember most
is the way she was a self-appointed assistant.

Little Heather is a big girl now
Probably married and a mother of two
I don't know
I haven't seen her since elementary school.

That was Little Heather
A tiny little girl
But one of the best students
In a teacher's world.

The following poem was not written by me, but it was written to me. I have enjoyed nearly all of my students over the years. Some I remember well, others hardly at all. This student enclosed a present with this poem. It was a silver necklace with a heart shaped pendant. I still have it in my possession to this day, just as I still have this poem. Who would have thought that it would appear in a book a few years later? Each student has his/her own story to tell. Here is Yuridia's story in short poem she wrote. I call this poem an Ode to a Teacher.

Ms Moore

By: Yarilia Zwceras

You're the best: #1 Teacher

Ms. Moore. is the moon.
Ms. Moore is the sun.
But she is the brightest.
of all the stars.

She is pretty & smart.
But sometimes she is kind of hard.

When she is sad,
Her students try to make. her gladd

I cry in tears
Because I want her to be the teacher of all
the years.

Excellent
Teacher

I love Ms Moore

Best
Teacher

Because she is the teacher of
all the World

I was inspired to write this poem because of my nephew, Larry, II and his friends. They are just regular Black boys growing up in America, The history of America and Black boys do not mix well; therefore, I worry about my nephew and his friends as they go places and do things that teenage boys do. It's a scary thought what could happen to these boys just for being boys…black boys. My nephew and his friends have made it through their first three hurdles in life… middle school, adolescence, and high school. They are now attending colleges of their choices and making a future for themselves. In the meantime, say a…

Prayer for Black Boys

Dear God,

Now I lay me down to sleep
I pray for Black Boys on the street.

I pray that they will make good choices
Let them hear their mamas' voices.

"Son, grow up and do what's right
I pray that you'll come home tonight.

You want to party and just have fun
but why do y'all have to carry those guns?"

From trouble, let them stray
avoid death, Lord, and die another day.

But if they die before I wake
I pray Lord their souls you should take.

Why do girls who make the cheering squad turn into cheering monsters? What happens to their original personality? Well, I had an opportunity to work with nine eighth grade cheerleaders, and they soon developed a personality I was not expecting. The unfortunate part is they had help turning against the cheerleader coach from one of my very own coworkers. Therefore, I call this poetic story *Cheering Squad Firing Squad.*

Cheering Squad Firing Squad

Here is the story of what I mean
Nine eighth grade girls made the cheering team

They started out just great
Eventually, their hearts turned to stone and hate

We practiced daily after school
Working on making our cheers extra cool

A co-worker wanted to volunteer
She raved about knowing how to cheer

Good, I could use the helping hand
Help the girls do the best they can.

Right away we didn't see eye to eye
She wanted to push MY ideas aside.

In my face she grinned
Behind my back she became a biting hen.

She told the girls things that I didn't know

Their attitude began to tell me so.

She raved about doing my job much better
Oh, she proclaimed to have better cheers...whatever.

They needed someone who knows how to cheer
This was a waste of their time this year.

Their innocent minds were sabotaged
They no longer came to practice with a willing heart.

Exactly what was wrong I couldn't readily surmise
Their aloof behavior came as a surprise.

They would not cheer and would not practice
They quit on purpose for spite and malice.

No matter what I did to get them on track
Her voice echoed behind my back.

My eighth grade cheering squad
Became my nightmare firing squad.

We stuck with it until the last game
I did nothing wrong, I had no shame.

I felt hurt and betrayed
That a co-worker would do me this way.

I rewarded the girls for doing their best
In spite of the undue disrespect.

I was an eighth grader when I wrote this poem the first time. I decided to write an adult remix.

Summer Fun Remix

Summer fun
is lying in the sun
drinking a fruit smoothie
and lying under a shady canopy.

Summer fun
is soaking up the sun
drinking an on-the-rocks martini
wearing a cute, colorful bikini

Summer fun
is tanning in the sun
lying under a palm tree
spying the male beach bodies you see.

Summer fun
is basking in the sun
eating melons, pineapples, and kiwi
going in and out of reality.

Actually, I have never been to a circus. I have never seen a clown. I have only seen clowns on television. I know the circus comes to town. All kinds of circuses: Universoul Circus, Big Top Circus, Barnum and Bailey Ringling Brothers, and Apple Circus. These are the most popular circuses that I know of, but I have never been to a circus.

I remember seeing an episode of a television show when one of the characters was the manager of a White singing artist. She wanted to sing a song about being a clown. She even dressed like a clown. The manager did not want her to sing that song; he thought the audience would not like it. She sang the song and was a hit with the audience. This is as much as I know about clowns. This poem is for my students. They need help understanding sensory details.

A Clown

I went to the circus
There I saw a clown
With a big white face
so sad and round.

His hair was a rainbow
as colorful as can be
I saw red, yellow, green,
and all colors for my eyes to see.

I went to the circus
There I saw a clown
Dressed in a big-balloon shirt
That looked like a gown.

Angellia Moore

It had colorful polka dots
Red, yellow, green, and blue
Looking like a bag of Skittles
Bright, colorful, and fun to chew

I went to the circus
There I saw a clown
With a sad smile, crying eyes
And an upside-down frown.

Once I saw a clown
As sad as can be
How can a sad clown
Make me smile and be happy?

The Worn out Chair is a poem I wrote for my students to help them understand sounds in literature.

The Worn Out Chair

The worn out chair

sits quietly in the corner

at least until someone

comes to sit on it.

When someone sits there,

the chair creaks and cracks

squeaks and squawks

until the big hips find their place.

The legs wobble and ricochet

from left to right

but it holds up until

the person goes away.

The poem that follows is a question poem. It is a poem that asks about our Mother Earth. I was inspired to write this poem in April for Earth Day. It was intended for young readers, but adults can appreciate a poem about out earthly home.

Who am I?

I am one of the nine orbiting planets.   Who am I?

I have trees and plants that provide oxygen for the whole world.   Who am I?

I have flowers that give fragrances and natural beauty for all to see.   Who am I?

I am covered in all kinds of soils that are dark, red, and sandy.   Who am I?

I give plenty of vegetables, grains, and fruit to everyone.   Who am I?

I need water on a regular basis for people, plants, and animals.   Who am I?

I give water to keep everything clean and green.   Who am I?

I make the world go round.   Who am I?

Don't forget; celebrate me every year in April.   Who am I?

Answer: Mother Earth

CHAPTER 2: Poetic Stories

from the Eyes of my

Soul

This is one of my favorite poems that I have written. I was inspired to write this poem because I often wonder how men see Black women. What exactly do they see when they look at us? Are they really attracted to us? Do they see the possibility of love when they look at a Black woman?

Mister, What Do You See?

Brown, green, hazel, and blue eyes looking at me
Tell me now Mister,
what do you see?

Black, brown, beige, and light skin
Do you wonder
who were my ancestral kin?

Natural hair, good hair, straight or curly hair
Do you wonder
how my goldilocks got there?

Phat lady, plump lady, tall slender or older lady
Do you see me,
a mama, with my beautiful baby?

Crying eyes, sad smile, longing stare, loving lips
Do you see
all this or just my curvy hips?

Talking loud, snapping fingers, popping neck
What's with
the drama that comes with all that?

Single, married, going through a divorce
Do you see
me as the future wife of your choice?

Diva, gold digger, drama queen, classy lady
Do you see
me as the mother of your little baby?

Brown, green, hazel and blue eyes looking at me
Tell me now Mister,
what do you see?

My inspiration for *I am My Own Flower* came on Sunday, a Mother's Day. I was preparing and getting ready for church. I was excited to wear a brand new white pants suit by Jones New York. I had a new blouse too that I just bought from a local department store. I especially liked the blouse because it made me feel feminine and pretty like a flower. I felt very lovely that Sunday as I went to church; therefore, *I am My Own Flower.*

I am My Own Flower

I am my own flower
a daisy or a daffodil
yellow and bright
just as the morning sun.

I am my own flower
a rose or a hibiscus
red and beautiful
just as Picasso's colorful oil painting.

I am my own flower
a hydrangea or an African violet
lavender and fresh
just as the morning dew.

I am my own flower
a carnation or a lily
white and strong
just as the inner soul.

I am my own flower
a gardenia or a honeysuckle
orange and fragrant
just as a bottle of perfume.

I am my own flower
a chrysanthemum or a tulip
pink and lovely
just like a graceful First Lady.

I am my own flower.

Ladies, you are your own flower too.

Write your own verses here.

_____

_____

_____

_____

_____

_____

Which way is up? What's up with that? What would Jesus do? What do you do when you have a million things on your mind? The tasks on that "To Do" list ache constantly in your mind until you do something about them. Something as simple as going to the store can ache in your mind until it's done. For example, if I am thinking about going to go to the local drug store, supermarket, or discount store, it aches in my mind until I get up and go. I may be waiting until the traffic dies down or I may be waiting until the sun sets a little. Whatever, I can't function or do anything else until I take care of the ache in my mind. Does this ever happen to you? Well, just do, but don't kill anyone.

Things on My Mind

Wake the kids
Make the bed
Start the day
Toast the bread

Off to work
Almost eight
Beat the traffic
Don't be late

Go to the bank
Cash the check
Money is gone
Ah, what the heck

Pay the bills
Pay by cash
Pay on line
No more money in the stash

Wash the clothes
Vacuum the floor
Dust the furniture
Dash to the store

Buy the groceries
Cook the food
Clean the kitchen
Take a break, fool

Love my man
Give him a squeeze
Splash on a fragrance
and a black nightie for tease

Have the baby
Nurse the child
Change the baby
Go the extra mile

Stop at the mall
Shop from store to store
Tired and ready to drop
Right at the door

The poem *I's Free, Now Leave Me Be* sounds like a line from a former slave. Of course, I am not a slave, never have been. I have been free all my life. This poem is dedicated to people who keep bugging me to cut, curl, trim, or put a chemical relaxer in my hair. I haven't always worn a natural hair style, but recently I had a battle with cancer. The chemotherapy medicine caused me to lose my hair. See, my hair is just now growing back after completing my chemotherapy treatments. I wore the wig for six months, and soon thereafter, my hair began to grow back. The locks of curls grew back fine, thin, and tight. Inch by inch it began to grow. After six months, it was a whopping three inches long. That's pretty good for my natural hair. As it began to grow, I felt a rebellion against using chemical relaxers. I did not want to use chemicals in it to relax the curls. So, I decided to leave my hair be. Some of my family members said cut it, trim it, shape it, curl it, and even relax it. I resisted, and I told them I would not do such a thing…at least not right now. My natural hair makes me feel free; therefore, I wrote this poem entitled *I's Free, Now Leave Me Be*. It has to do with the state of my natural Black hair.

I's Free, Now Leave Me Be

I's free
now leave me be
no more chemicals
in my hair for me.

I's free
now leave me be
I'm letting my hair
grow out naturally.

I's free
now leave me be
thick curls, dreadlocks, afro
feeling so free

Angellia Moore

I's free
now leave me be
my hair is growing
as God intended naturally.

I was inspired to write this poem because a friend of mine always makes a reference to a person's outer beauty. For example, if we are watching the news and the anchor tells the story of a thug criminal (male or female) who is on the street stealing, killing, robbing or using drugs, he would always mention the physical look of the person. "She is such a pretty lady." "He is a good-looking guy." I would hit the ceiling and ask what does it matters how the person looks? A criminal is a criminal. A drug addict is a drug addict. A thug is a thug no matter how he or she looks. Therefore, *Beauty Doesn't Matter.*

Beauty Doesn't Matter

Beauty doesn't matter
when you are lonely.

Beauty doesn't matter
when you are hurting.

Beauty doesn't matter
when you don't feel loved.

Beauty doesn't matter
when you are heading to divorce court.

Beauty doesn't matter
when abuse creeps in.

Beauty doesn't matter
when your child is in trouble.

Angellia Moore

Beauty doesn't matter
when drugs take over.

Beauty doesn't matter
when you become a desperate criminal.

Beauty doesn't matter
when a jail cell becomes your home

Beauty doesn't matter
when sickness or disease takes over you.

Beauty doesn't matter
when you die.

One of my students died. He was a boy of about 10 years old. One day after school, he got off the bus and was walking home. He saw a big rig parked in his neighborhood. I supposed that in his head, he decided to take a short cut to his house. The short cut was to go under the big rig and cut across the parking lot. Just as the little boy was crawling under the rig, the driver began to move his truck. Unknowingly to the driver, an innocent child decided to take an alternate route home under the vehicle. The child was crushed to an instant and untimely death. Many people were heartbroken and emotionally distraught. So was I; therefore, I wrote this poem, *An Angel Again*, for the family and for my own form of dealing with grief. No child should die like this.

An Angel Again

As I lay awake that night
not able to sleep.
I prayed to God that
All of us would find peace.

A peace that would comfort
and give each one rest.
A peace that lets you know
He is with the absolute best.

For he was an angel here on earth
who touched the hearts of many.
He was the sweetest little boy,
The nicest and kindest of any!

He is an angel again,
A spirit now gone far above.
He is warmly embraced and received
By God's bountiful and everlasting love.

Father, mother, sister, and brothers
you are a sweet and loving family.
Thank you for allowing us
to share in your love for Avery.

May God bless each of you
one by one and…together.
I pray that love, joy, peace, kindness,
goodness, and gentleness will be with you forever.

Your son, a beautiful child, son, brother,
classmate, student, and friend
He was an angel before,
and he is an angel again.

February 15, 1998

I remember, as teenagers, my cousin and I used to walk back and forth from her mother's house to my mother's house. We lived only about a quarter of a mile from each other. We rode the same bus (#67), and we went to the same high school. Of course, one day these two teenager girls grew up and went their separate ways. I went to college; she got married. For many years our paths seldom crossed.

In the last couple of years of her life, our paths crossed again. She sent me a message by a family member *"To come see her the next time I was home."* I was home when I got the message, so I did just that. I drove a quarter of a mile to go see her this time instead of walking. At that time neither one of us knew we had cancer. We laughed and talked and caught up to the current times. The next couple of years brought anxiety and fear to both of us. We found out around the same time that we both had cancer. Her cancer was different from mine. I was diagnosed with breast cancer. She had bone cancer. The inevitable happened. Recently, my cousin, my friend died of cancer. She lost her battle with cancer on February 26. This poem was written especially for her.

A Better Place

We often think this world is it
A place we don't want to leave,
but God says, "There is a better place
child, come join me, if you please".

"Come to heaven, my dear
Come to a far better place
A place many others want to go
you are fortunate to see my glory and grace."

A dearly beloved mother,
daughter, sister, aunt, cousin, coworker, and friend
She gave us her all and all
Right up to the very end.

We are glad for the memories we have
Her shining eyes, bright smile, and affectionate call, "Baby"
God put us here with her
for such a time as this…. just maybe.

Our paths may have diverged
some of us went to the left; some went to the right,
God gave us a spiritual connection
to bring us together when the time was right.

God allowed us to come together
Hugs and laughs we had
Sharing old times and new times
So, we mustn't be too sad.

We lost a beautiful sheep from here on earth
Surely, we will miss her giggles and smiling face,
but God says, "My dear, come,
Come with me to a better place."

Heaven is always a better place!
We love you, Edna Carol
February 26, 2010

Look into my eyes. Come closer. Can you see her, Anne? She is leaning forward with her hands on her knees. She has a smile on her face. She is a tall and thin teenager. She is wearing a red round-neck body shirt with skin-tight blue jeans. Her wavy black hair is pulled back into a fluffy- puffy ponytail. Are you able to see her in your mind? That's the Anne this poetic story is about. Anne died twenty four years ago. I can't remember the date. I never saw the obituary. I was a young college graduate and just starting to earn money as a teacher. I was not financially able to attend her funeral in New York, so I did not get to see my first best friend one last time.

I haven't talked about Anne in years. Then, one day I saw a high school classmate who remembered that Anne and I were best friends. She asked me, "Whatever happened to Anne Little?" I shared her fate with them, and here's the story of my first best friend, Anne.

Anne

Anne and I grew up side by side
Starting in elementary school at grade five.

She moved to NC from New York
She was prim and proper in her talk.

We met and became fast friends
I was with her until the very end.

We were two shy little girls
Growing up in a small-town world.

She was endearing and funny
She made our friendship sunny.

Anne had a different maturity than me
I was just a country girl, you see.

She teased me about my funny face
I was the first one to welcome her in a new place.

This is where I understood best friends
Which we were until her end.

She and I had a kindred connection
A friendship full of perfection.

We laughed and talked
Our booties bumped when we walked.

We had crushes on high school boys
We grew out of playing with silly toys.

"Don't take any wooden nickels," she always said
To this day that phrase is stuck in my head.

But she wasn't happy living in the south
She was adamant about getting out.

Soon after high school graduation
Her bags were packed, and she was at the Greyhound station.

Anne was New York bound
She was vacating this little hick town.

My first best friend, Anne, moved away
Then she up and died one day.

Anne found out she was sick
At that time, she was only twenty-six.

She died from a respiratory disease
It was hard for her to breathe.

New York was not good for her life
Too much stress and too much strife.

I wanted her to move out of the city
But she loved the Big Apple, a good and plenty.

In my last conversation with Anne
I shared my move-her-out-of New York plan.

I was too late, but she heard my cry
Unfortunately, life soon thereafter passed her by.

I lost my first best friend
But never her memories embedded within.

I have nothing much to remember Anne
No pictures, no letters, no relatives, a blank hand.

But I can see her smiling face
Embedded in my mind, her final resting place.

My first best friend
Ardelia Anne Little and her untimely end.

Once, not long ago, I bought a beautiful, single-band 18k gold flex bracelet. The suggested retail price was $699.99, but I purchased it for about 50% off. To me this was expensive. It was designed with more of a bangle style that just wraps around the arm, no clasp. On either ends of the band was a miniature size ball of *Swarovski Crystals*. I declared in my mind, that was a beautiful bracelet.

At first, I couldn't wear it. It was too elegant to wear to work; therefore, I kept it in its original package tucked away. So, there it set for days, weeks, months. Periodically, I would take it out just to admire it. One day, I decided to wear it to work, what the heck. I received so many compliments on that bracelet. So, I just began to wear it anytime.

I had a special trip and event coming up, so I decided to buy the same bracelet again to amplify its beauty. I just knew two of the same bracelets would look lovely together. I went back to the same store and bought the same bracelet. Now, I had two exquisite 18k gold flex bracelets with Swarovski Crystal balls on either ends to take on my trip out of town that was coming up very soon. To my next event, I would wear these bracelets. Thus, this is the story of the Swarovski Crystal bracelets.

The 14k Gold Swarovski *CRYSTALLIZED* Flex Bracelets

Last summer, in June
On the road I would be soon.

My clothes, shoes, and bracelet in tow
Two gold flex bangles for show.

I arrived at my destination
I was happy with much elation.

My bracelets I wore on my right arm
Their beauty was such a striking charm.

My hostess raved about their beauty
She wanted one from me immediately.

47

I didn't volunteer to give her mine
I thought, I'll give her one next time.

The whole time of my visit there
She coveted and looked at them with care.

On my last day to leave,
Hold on, this you won't believe.

We went to church for worship
Singing and clapping, I was immersed.

Then a still small quiet voice said
"Give her the bracelet." I heard it in my head.

I gasped with shock and surprise.
"Right now?" I asked to my demise.

Yes, you have two
Give her one and keep one for you.

I had to come to terms
Obedience was one of my first lessons learned.

I took the gold bracelet off and gave it to Bren
She is and has always been a good friend.

I resolved with God and my inner me
This I know was certainly meant to be.

She was some kind of elated
That14k Gold Swarovski *CRYSTALLIZED* Bracelet was highly over-rated.

Today, I am totally at peace in parting with one of those 14k Gold Swarovski *CRYSTALLIZED* Flex Bracelets. I figured, if I did not give it to Bren, then someone else would have coveted it just as much, and I would have to give it to that person. As a matter of fact, every time I wear the single bracelet I still have, someone comments on how beautiful it is. Currently, it is in the package and tucked away. At the same time, I am glad God used me in this special way.

DAZZLING DEAL! Gold 'N' Ice Crystal Bangle 14K

$279.60
Original $699.00

Only genuine crystals can deliver such sensational sparkle. This 14k bangle glistens with round crystals.

Metal: 14K gold
Metal Color: Yellow
Stones: *CRYSTALLIZED*™ - Swarovski Elements
Closure: Flex bangle

Jewelry photos are enlarged to show detail.

Item Number: FC296-2160

1   quantity

click the box to add ...
☐ Lifetime Jewelry Care Plan for $64.99

The Principal brings to my mind a principal I once worked under. I admired her then, and I admire her to this day.

The Principal

Once I had a principal

As stately as can be

She walked with a tall stature

A proud principal for everyone to see.

A tall beautiful lady

As classy as they come

Walking around the school building

To the beat of her very own drum.

She was always in a hurry

Going nowhere fast

Just making her way around

To each and every class.

I was a beginning teacher

Happy and quite energized

Building my career path

She nicknamed me *Bright Eyes.*

When she saw me in the hall

"Ms. Moore," she would say

"How are you

and your little babies today?"

I have had several principals

None quite like her

Full of decorum and etiquette

She was always so prim, always so proper.

Meticulous in her style and dress

Meticulous in how and what she ate

around her one learned how to teach

and one learned how to be a lady.
In fine stores she shopped
Buying the finest clothes and leather shoes
from Nordstrom, Ann Taylor, and Neiman Marcus
Designer names I didn't have money to choose.
I learned a lot from this principal of distinction
From how and what she would say
To the way she carried herself
Her life-lessons still linger with me today.

CHAPTER 3: Poetic Stories

From the Eyes of my

Consciousness

There is so much going on around us. How do we keep our sanity with so many Societal Woes?

Societal Woes

Societal woes pulling us left and right
Making it hard to keep God in sight

Not sure of what's right and wrong
Hip hop, R & B, Pop, everybody singing a different song

Po' folks living on the street
People dying right at your feet

Economic pressures making people holler
American citizens squeezing the almighty dollar

Planes dashing and crashing from the sky
Wild police chases going by

Wiping noses from influenza and sneezes
Dying young from sicknesses and diseases

Reality Shows on every television dial
Sex in the city and girls going wild

Families breaking down or breaking up
What the hell, just giving up!

Couples giving up on marriage for a divorce
Setting their lives on a different course

Black men crossing the track
Black women can't get 'em back

Baby girls having babies
Forgetting about being young ladies

Young boys taking what's not theirs
Killing and stealing without any cares

Preachers preaching prosperity and wealth
Leaving out poor folks with failing health

Illegal drug trafficking is still a fight
Police breaking down doors and shining lights

Gang banging is a national crime
Killing each other on a dime

Immigrants trying to come in
The law putting them out again

Homosexual relationships coming out
Heterosexuals treading on doubt

Societal woes breaking us apart
'Cause love ain't in the depths of our heart.

You think?

This poem, *Knuckleheads are People Too,* is inspired from a saying that is a part of my colloquial speech. Also, I hear other people saying this too. When you start judging others for who they are, making generalizations, or stereotyping people just remember they are people too. Every family has some type of knucklehead among them. *Knuckleheads are People Too* is an interactive poem. I need for you to fill in the blank, in the second poem, with the name of the human rights group that you are passionate about or that you find yourself judging.

Knuckleheads are People Too!

Knuckleheads are People Too
Life treats them the same as you

Knuckleheads are People Too
No matter what they say or do

Knuckleheads are People Too
They are sensitive with feelings too

Knuckleheads are People Too
Family and friends love them, true.

Knuckleheads are People Too
They too want love and a Sweet Bu

Knuckleheads are People Too
Shedding tears because they are blue

Knuckleheads are People Too
Depression strikes them, me, even you

Knuckleheads are People Too
Some are in left field without a clue

Knuckleheads are People Too
Their radical/odd behavior is nothing new

Angellia Moore

Knuckleheads are People Too
Spreading germs and catching the flu

Knuckleheads are People Too
They sneeze, and we say bless you

Knuckleheads are People Too
They drink, eat, and chew

Knuckleheads are people Too
They want respect just like you.

Knuckleheads are People Too
Born to live and born to die too

Knuckleheads are people too.

Now, you try it. Fill in the name of the group you feel strongly about.

_____ are People Too!
_____ are People Too
Life treats them the same as you

_____ are People Too
No matter what they say or do

_____ are People Too
They are sensitive with feelings too

_____ are People Too
Family and friends love them, true.

_____ are People Too
They too want love and a sweet Boo

_____ are People Too
Shedding tears because they are blue

_____ are People Too

Depression strikes them, me, even you

_____ are People Too
Some are in left field without a clue

_____ are People Too
Their radical/odd behavior is nothing new

_____ are People Too
Spreading germs and catching the flu

_____ are People Too
They sneeze, and we say bless you

_____ are People Too
They drink, eat, and chew

Knuckleheads are people Too
They want respect just like you

_____ are People Too
Born to live and born to die too

_____ are people too.

The poem, *One Minuscule Man,* reads like a negative poem against men, but it really isn't a negative arrow pointed toward men. It just amazes me how one small, petite, thin, minuscule man weighing 180 pounds can make a decision in his head that can change other people's plans, can change the history in the making, a family's dynamic, the world we live in. We all live and die at the risk of *One Minuscule Man.*

One Minuscule Man

One minuscule man
Lurks with a gun in hand
Shooting down the other man
and away he ran.

One minuscule guy
With fire and death in his eye
Gonna live or gonna die
Sneaking past life, barely getting by.

One minuscule bro'
Didn't want to let the sista go
Put a gun to her head, and so
took her life—now you know.

One minuscule athlete
Tells the other woman she is sweet
Sweeps her off her feet
Now, he's known as a cheat.

One minuscule dude
Acting like he's cool
On the streets playing pool
Shooting up drugs like a fool.

Angellia Moore

One minuscule wimp
Drives by for a glimpse
Target view becomes a blimp
Gun goes off and leaves a man limp.

One minuscule thug
Friend to alcohol and drugs
Police lineup and police mug
The way of life for a thug.

One minuscule leader
A president, governor, or preacher
Raises his hand in oath as our leader
Can't get it right neither.

One minuscule man

Wreaking havoc across the land

Taking lives in his own hand

All because he thinks he can.

That one minuscule man

Take a walk in your neighborhood. Take a walk in the park. Take a walk in the big hustling and bustling city. Listen to the sounds around you. What do you hear, the noises of life? Start out one morning as early as you can. Walk through your neighborhood or Local Park, meditate and enjoy the noises of life, at least the good ones.

Noises of Life

Honk, honk

Beep, beep!

"Taxi!"

Vroom, vroom a city bus pulls off

City Streets

Boom, boom,

Pow!

Ha, ha, ha, ha!

Thump, thump, thump

Yeah, wow, the crowd yells

A Family Reunion

Tweet, tweet!

Chirp, chirp!

Scurry, scurry!

Zoom, zoom, an airplane goes by

A walk in the park.

"I said no!"

"Stop, you're hurting me."

Smack!

"Stop!"

Angellia Moore

Smack, Smack

"What I tell you?"

Whine, Whine, a baby cries

A violent household.

"Stop, Police!"

Pow! Pow!

Pop, pop!

Thump,

"Ah" a criminal dies

Night Streets

"Mom!"

Spongebob Square Pants

"Gimme that!"

Honey, I'm home!"

Dinner is ready yells mom from the kitchen

A loving home.

Can you relate to this poem, *Outta Shape*? I can. One spring day I found myself out of shape. I could hardly wear my clothes, and they were nice clothes too. I felt embarrassed and ashamed of the weight on my hips and the bulge around my waist. My blouses were bulging open and my pants went up one size. I also discovered the culprit of my blubbering belly. It is called sugar, excessive calories, and not enough exercise. Dieticians or health gurus say your caloric intake should not exceed 2000 per day. I say that is way too many. In order to get rid of the weight and get in shape, a woman in her right mind needs to significantly decrease the calories taken in her body and exercise at least 60 minutes a day. Here is one fact I found in my daily exercise routine, it takes five minutes of movement to dissolve 25 calories in the body. So, get moving because you are *Outta Shape* too.

Outta Shape

A glance in the mirror
A quick side view
Shake your head in disgust
At the shape and size of you.
    Outta Shape

A fat flabby belly
Bouncing boobs, muffing top roll
Big thick booty
Everywhere there's a crease and a fold.
    Outta Shape

Hurting knees
Chafing and rubbing thighs
Aching feet
All you can do is sigh.
    Outta Shape

Pants too tight
Can't get 'em past the hips
Zipper won't budge
Suck in the air from the lips.
      Outta Shape

Heart racing
Thumping out of your chest
Lungs full of air
Gasping and out of breath.
      Outta Shape

Gotta start out slow
One step at a time
Get that weight off
Soon you'll be fine.
      Outta Shape
Mind made up
15 minutes will do
Get started, keep moving
Do it for you.
      Outta Shape

Increase time to thirty minutes
Pounding the street
Taking deep breaths
And beating the heat.
      Outta Shape

Up to 60 minutes now, good
Walking hard, walking steady
With rhythmic breathing
Now you are ready.
        Outta Shape

Shapely figure returning
Pants and skirt now fit
Thinning waist line
Outta shape no more, but a hit.
            Yeah, you are Outta Shape too

Ticket Out of Poverty

Raise your hand high
If you know a place called poverty.
Many of us grew up there;
poor, desolate, desperate, disengaged
Looking for a ticket out of poverty
Hoping to go elsewhere.

Raise your hand high
If you know a place called poverty.
Trying to get out of there
Working, struggling, saving
Looking for a ticket out of poverty
Hoping to go somewhere.

Raise your hand high
If you know a place called poverty.
Single mothers live there
Angry, crying, praying
Looking for a ticket out of poverty
Hoping to go anywhere.

Raise your hand high
If you know a place called poverty.
Husbands and fathers live there
Looking for work, trying to make a dollar, a job will do
Looking for a ticket out of poverty
Hoping for a better life elsewhere.

Raise your hand high
If you know a place called poverty.
Poor, helpless, children live there
Crying, begging, pleading
Looking for a ticket out of poverty
Hoping there is help out there somewhere.

Raise your hand high
If you know a place called poverty.
Many of us grew up there
Lack of education, minimum wages, taking risks
Looking for a ticket out of poverty
Hoping for opportunities out there.

Raise your hand high
If you knew a place called poverty.
Don't want to live there
Longing, hoping to making it out
Finding your ticket out of poverty
Life is going somewhere.

One day, I decided that life as I knew it was not what I wanted anymore. I was tired of the same ole' same ole' things in life. I believed on the inside of me that there had to be more than this, than what I was experiencing. So, I made my plans to make the biggest move I have ever made. I decided to move to Georgia from Virginia. I only knew about three people there, but that was enough. I did my homework on checking out job perspectives, and I found a school district that appealed to my financial needs. I boxed up my belongings, hired some movers, and drove the eight hours south to the Metro-Atlanta area. Thus, here I am in Georgia.

When I first got here, I thought that it was odd that people purposely segregated themselves. It seemed to me that certain people lived here and certain other races of people lived there, and others lived over there. It was what they wanted. It works.

Quiet Segregation

I moved to the Deep South about five years ago
The surrounding atmosphere was different at best
It seemed to me there was a quiet segregation
Seemingly, a quiet segregation at rest.

Quiet segregation after all these years
Fills the Deep South
Sh, sh, sh, sh hush!
You didn't hear it from my mouth.

Certain people live on the south side
Others live in the north and west
But the people with the money
Live in places called the best.

Angellia Moore

A quiet segregation
A civil and a quiet rest
Nobody is protesting
There is no civil unrest.

In their own way, people are nice
People are kind
Unspoken it is said you stay in your place
and I'll stay in mine.

I like the Deep South
heat, traffic, and all…go figure
People don't bother you
or call you the N word, nigger.

Sure, many of us suffer with a little bit of self-esteem issues. One may think he/she is too skinny or too fat. Others may see themselves as not very beautiful for one reason or another. Many people have heard these comments somewhere in their lives. I fall into the first stanza category. Stand up for your beauty no matter what form it comes. State it emphatically.

I Ain't Ugly!

You call me names,
like red and dirty red
You call me skinny
Everything but a nappy head.
I ain't ugly!

You call me fat,
big, and out of shape.
You call me something
close to an ape.
I ain't ugly!

You call me big nose,
but butt, and big feet
You call me cross-eyed
snaggle tooth and buck teeth
I ain't ugly!

You call me darkie
blue, midnight, jet black.
You call me that cause
you were born on the other side of the track.
I ain't ugly!

Angellia Moore

You call me somebody's love child

Illegitimate, born out of wed lock, daddy's maybe

You call me a shameful name,

I wonder if I'm daddy's baby.

I ain't ugly!

You call me tall

Heavy duty, with big bones.

You call me a giant

Your words make me feel alone.

I ain't ugly!

You call me that n word

Niggard, nigger, negro

You call me a nothing

but I say it ain't so.

I ain't ugly!

You can call me pretty
my inner beauty shining through
You call me pleasingly plump
my outer beauty is quite striking too.
'cause I ain't ugly!

You notice my smile
My teeth ain't straight.
One's broke and one's gone
Dental care came too late.
I ain't ugly!

You call me Po' Trash
My poverty is all you see
Skin and bones, dingy, tattered clothes
All you do is stare at me.
I ain't ugly!

This is just the way I see society. These are our everyday issues that we face day in and day out.

An Explanation

Once it was taxation

without representation.

Now it's frustration

followed by desperation.

Talk about hateration

forget about collaboration.

Today's U. S. population

exploding from immigration.

Never ending altercations

street violence and annihilation.

The now generation

making their societal donation.

Electronic (e-) socialization

ending global separation.

Legal arbitration

court and credit intimidation.

Past segregation

still working on integration.

Packed congregations

fulfilling spiritual relations.

Outlandish imagination

all kinds of new creations.

Good education

bringing illumination.

American celebration

living in a Democratic nation.

Need clarification

Just giving you an explanation.

Sometimes in life we just have to bite the bullet, go with the flow, or in this case, *Swallow that Chunky Pill*. We may not like everything going on around us, but change is inevitable. There are so many modern-day changes coming our way that we need to get used to them. Some pills are just hard to swallow especially the bigger ones. They seem to not go down; they just get lodged in your throat, so is the way of life as we know it today.

Swallow that Chunky Pill

A Black President on Capitol Hill
Swallow that chunky pill.
Congress passing an immigration Bill
Swallow that chunky pill.
Immigrants keeping it real
Swallow that chunky pill.
Interracial lovers the new big deal
Swallow that chunky pill.
No more texting at the wheel
Swallow that chunky pill.
Life is just run-of-the mill
Swallow that chunky pill.
Bang, bang! Shoot to kill
Swallow that chunky pill.
Children going without a meal
Swallow that chunky pill.
Can't say, "God or peace be still"
Swallow that chunky pill.
We need to say "God's will"
Swallow that chunky pill.

A few years ago, I decided to move to Georgia, the Metro-Atlanta area. I was excited and spell bound by the magnitude and vastness of the area. As I was contemplating my big move to Georgia, I visited the area and returned a couple of times for interviews and apartment hunting. It was a bright and beautiful spring day. The sky was a clear blue with white cumulus clouds. Just so happened, that while I was in the area, I saw a young lady driving a green convertible BMW on the parkway. I thought to myself, *Cool, I want to be like that when I move here.* Well, I have moved here.

Fly Girl Going By

Once I saw a fly girl going by
Her green convertible BMW caught my eye.

She was a beautiful brown fly girl
Rolling along in her own fly world.

She zoomed down the Sugarloaf Parkway
Arm out the window, as if to say "hey!"

She quickly zoomed out of sight
but my mind's camera clicked it just right.

Her freedom and fly-ness inspired me
To be all that I can one day be.

Today, you'll see another fly girl going by
Maybe her black convertible SLRA will catch your eye.

She is a beautiful brown fly girl
Rolling along in her own fly world.

You'll see her zooming down the same parkway
Arm out the window, wave and just say "hey!"

Have you ever felt anxious about something that is looming in your future? I know I have. I feel anxious, jittery, and almost restless, especially when I am looking forward to something special. Then it came to me, walk through life, don't run. There is too much goodness to see and partake of.

Walk, Don't Run

Walk, don't run

Smell the dozens of red, pink, and yellow roses

lovely fragrances right under your noses.

Walk, don't run

Feel the warm, radiant sun rays basking against your skin

Relax, breathe, and take it all in.

Walk don't run

Admire the gigantic, lush, beautiful, and green trees

Stop, stare, and just freeze.

Walk, don't run

Listen closely to the rushing river and the sound of peace

Filling your heart with spiritual belief.

Walk, don't run

Be reminded that life is too short

Be athletic, walk, and take it to the court.

Walk, don't run

Discover the many undiscovered places out there

Take a trip somewhere… anywhere.

Walk, don't run

There is still too much to understand

Don't let this be your last plan.

Walk, don't run

Go to a few of the thousands of places to see

Go and give of you generously.

Angellia Moore

Walk, don't run

Do a few of the thousands of things to do

Have some fun and just be you.

Walk, don't run

Meet and make new diverse friends

They will last until life's end.

Walk, don't run

Your destiny in life remains the same

Anyway you get there, it doesn't change.

Walk, don't run

I know there is a thin line between sanity and insanity. I promise you that I am not suffering with a mild case of insanity. So, when you read the next poem, *The Invisible Hand*, read it in its entirety before making any harsh judgments. I kept having this recurring dream about a room that I was afraid to go into. My insides would quiver at the thought of going in that room. Just getting close to that room there was an eerie presence that met me in the pit of my stomach. It took *The Invisible Hand* to put me in a position to face that underlying fear of fear itself.

The Invisible Hand

The invisible hand came
again during the night.
Ever present in my room
giving me such a terrific fright.
So, I opened my eyes.

I did not want to go
into that room behind the door.
I could not go in it
that room frightened me even more.
So, I opened my eyes.

The invisible hand pushed me
forward, slowly, forward in my back.
Stone cold trepidation
held me steadfast in my tracks.
So, I opened my eyes.

My body began to quake
My mouth wanted to scream.
A small shriek came out
It ended that dream.
So, I opened my eyes.

Panic was on my face
Fear and fright were in my body
Get it off me
Help me please, somebody.
So, I opened my eyes.

Fear gripping my mind
Fear gripping my soul
Holding on to me
Like a suction cup's tight hold.
So, I opened my eyes.

The invisible hand came
leading me to face that fear.
Held squarely to face it
with the invisible hand so near.
So, I opened my eyes.

Not realizing it was there
inside, a seed buried so deep.
Torn up by the root
usually kept me from sleep.
So, I opened my eyes.

All this time, a fear of failure
or a fear of success
Holding on to me and
keeping me from doing my best.
So, I opened my eyes.

The invisible hand didn't come
I lay down and my eyes slowly closed.
No more inner fears
No more struggles to withhold.
So, I didn't open my eyes.

Places of Peace are places I have never physically been to, however, they are places that I go to mentally to get away from it all. They bring such a quietness and relaxation for the mind, the soul, and the body. These are places we would love to go to and just find peace waiting there. Tuck these *Places of Peace* away in your mind. When you need them, just go there for a few minutes.

Places of Peace

Take a little journey with me
down a long, narrow but straight road
bright sunshine at your back
a clear blue sky overhead.
nothing but green land in the distance
no rushing, honking cars
no hustling, bustling people
just the serenity of the earth, a place of peace.

Walk with me
to a cool, breezy ocean front
where the setting sun falls
behind the water's edge
sit there on the beach shore
facing the cool, dark water
waves crashing, dashing back and forth
sweet gentle breeze of the night air, a place of peace.

Come on, the quaint little cottage
sits in the middle of a beautiful yard
carpeted with thick green grass
wrapped in a white picket fence
a huge bushy-top oak tree

full and perfectly shading the yard
a gentle breeze rustles the leaves
another tree with a garden swing
a perfect place of peace.

The glorious garden awaits you
cool, green, and alive
with plants and natural noises
the sound of rushing and falling water
sunlight shining through the crevices
hitting your face just right
to warm you up in the garden
free to think or not, a place of peace.

The Important Thing

Have you discovered lately
That the most important thing
Isn't really all that important?
It may be important to you
At that particular time and place
After that, it's not so important any more.
What's important to you
Certainly may not be important to me
Who cares and life goes on.
You work hard for the important thing
Toiling day and night for achievement
and the thrill is gone shortly thereafter.
Nobody remembers the day
When the important thing was so important
It's long gone and forgotten.
Tomorrow holds a new set of important things
Things important to you and things important to me
Therefore, the most important thing
is important only for a little while.

CHAPTER 4: Poetic Stories

from the Eyes of my

Family and Friends

I am not even a mother, but I have a motherly instinct or a parental nod. I have worked with children all of my adult life as a teacher of elementary and middle school students. They are my favorite groups of children, and I respect and treat them just as they are my own children. I have a host of nieces and nephews, whom I love dearly. They look up to me and seek me for advice and counsel. I even housed several of them in a two bedroom apartment when they graduated from high school and were trying to find their way in life; no cost to them.

I was inspired to write this poem for my sister. She asked me to write a few short poems for her newsletter. I said okay, and I got really excited about writing for her newsletter. I wrote this Mother's Day acrostic poem in honor of Mother's Day. The first line of this poem is inspired from a song written by Pastor Shirley Caesar.

From a Mother's Heart

M   for the nine **months** I carried you, no cost

O   for the food **on** your plate, no cost

T   for the **time** I spent holding you, no cost

H   for the million **hugs** I've given you, no cost

E   for **each** and **every** birthday we celebrated, no cost

R'   for the **real** love I give to you unconditionally, no cost

S   for the **Sundays** I took you to church, no cost

      It's all from a mother's heart.

D   for the **days** and nights I sat up with you, no cost.

A   for the **active** role I play in your life, no cost.

Y   for the **years** I spent caring for you, no cost.

      It's all from a mother's heart.

Don't' be a deadbeat child. Do things for and with your mother, because every day with her counts. Below is a list of easy tasks that you can do with or for your mother and your father.

Celebrating Mother
Things to do for your Mother from A to Z

a	add up all the favors you owe her
b	buy her a bouquet of flowers, now
c	cook a meal for her, breakfast, lunch, or dinner; it doesn't matter
d	drive her to the doctor's office
e	eat dinner with her during the week
f	fix things around her house
g	give her a few extra dollars
h	hang out with her for a little while
i	include her in your plans
j	join your sisters and brothers and do your part
k	kiss her on the cheek
l	love her everyday
m	mow the lawn weekly
n	never bring hurt, harm, or danger to her
o	open an account just for her
p	pray for or with her daily
q	quit mooching off of yo' mama
r	respect here as your mother
s	sow spiritual seeds in her life
t	take good care of the one and only mother you have
u	use the time with her wisely
v	visit her often
w	write out her bills, buy the stamps, and mail the bills
x	'xercise with her
y	yield to her words of wisdom
z	zip your mouth and listen to your mother

This is the story of my own mother. I wrote this poem for her and about her approximately four years ago for one of our annual family gatherings. Yes, my mother had 10 children. I am number seven. Am I lucky or what? This poem has the rhythmic pattern of the *Old Lady who lived in the Shoe*. I cannot remember if I read this poem to my mother, but here it is.

MOTHER'S DELIGHT
(Mother's Day 2006)

Once there was a young lady
who lived in a house the size of a shoe.

She had ten bouncy children
And she didn't know what to do.

She said to herself

"Oh well, I'll raise them like I should
And hope they'll all grow up and be good."

The years passed and the children grew
Mother looked up and instantly knew

That she had raised them right
for ten children are now Mother's Delight.

I was commissioned to write this poem or at least a poem to honor fathers on Father's Day for a local newsletter. *I'm Glad to have a Dad* is written from a child's perspective, but who wouldn't be glad to have a dad around? I am one of the many kids in the United States who grew up without my father in the home. But I am okay. I think I turned out just fine. This is what came to me

I'm Glad to have a Dad
(from the voice of a child)

Dad picked me up when I was three.
Dad plays on the lawn with me.

Dad fixed my broken toy.
Dad loves me whether I am a girl or a boy.

Dad read books to me at night.
Dad says I am his delight.

Dad bought me clothes and shoes.
Dad buys me candy and food.

Dad took me places.
Dad brightens up our faces.

Dad celebrated my first day.
Dad is here with me today.

Dad, you must know I'm glad
to have you as my Dad.

Happy Dad's Day!

We are getting ready to celebrate my mother's 80th birthday. So, I wrote this poem as a tribute for her at her birthday bash. She says, *"You all are always telling my age."* Even at 80 years of age, there is still vanity. So, you did not hear it from me.

Virtuous Mother

Who can find a virtuous mother?
For her price is far above, sapphires, diamonds, and pearls
She is one that is like no other.
She is the family's best girl.

Her heart goes to her children.
They do trust in her deeply
For them she will do good not evil
She cherishes them completely.

She cleans the house, cooks everybody's favorite food
She works willingly with her hands
She is like a merchant
as she lays out her financial plans.

She rises early, preparing for the day
while it is still night
Planning a meal, cooking a breakfast
and breakfast is ready as soon as it gets light.

These things I remember
of our virtuous mother during our growing up years
We were just kids, running and playing
Without any cares and fears.

Mother would rise early
Off to work she went,
but breakfast was fixed first
That time was well spent.

Mother worked hard
Scraping to bring home a weekly pay check
Making ends meet
With a small salary such as that.

She paid her monthly bills
Bought sacks of groceries each week
She kept clean clothes on our back
and shoes on our feet.

Never did we go without a meal
Never did we go without lights
Mother knew what to do,
although money was really tight.

Today, mother still prepares for us
She sweeps, she cleans, and she bakes pies
Just like a mother hen
Anxiously waiting for us to arrive.

She is always glad to see us
She hates to see us go
She gets sad and lonely
A lonesome tear might show.

Her family is still her pride and joy
Each one very dear to her heart
She loves all of us
The sign of a virtuous mother by far.

Who can write a song and not write about a friend? Who can write a book and not speak of their friendships? Who can star in a movie and not have a best friend? How can I write a book of poetic stories about events, people, and places in my life and not write about my wonderful friends? Certainly, I am inspired by the many wonderful friendships I have made over the years. My memories take me from my first best friend of long ago to my new friends today. Some friends I regularly keep in touch with and some I can only think of. Capturing the essence of all my friends would require a longer work and would need to be a book in itself. So, I tried to capture all of my friends in the poem *Alphabet Friends*. They are all special and hold a special place in my heart and mind.

Alphabet Friends

Friends connect when they are young
Friends gather when they are old
Friends keep precious memories,
stories, and secrets untold.

Friends become special people
Interacting in your life
Weaving different friendship patterns
and soothing your stresses and strife.

Friends become long-time comrades
Some since the young age of ten
Cousins, classmates, coworkers, sisters, brothers
the start of the list of Alphabet Friends.

Alphabet friends begin with A

Ann

Anne, Annie

Annette, Ardelia Ann, Aurica

Barbara

Betty, Brenda

Candice

Carisa, Cassandra

Celestine, Cheryl, Connie

Constance, Crystal, Curtis

Danielle

Darlene, Debra,

Denise, Detrich, Delorse

Deric, Derek, Derrick, Donald, Donna

Edna

Edith, Elsie, Erma

Felicia, Flora

Gloria, Greg

Harold, Harriet

Inez, Izzy

Jacquelyn,

James, Jarvis, Jeff

Jeffrey, Jennifer, Joyce

Karen

Karl, Keith

Kenneth

Laurie

Larry, Linda, Lisa

Margaret

Mary, Melvin

Michelle, Minerva, Miriam

Neat-Neat

Oggy, Ojerie

Pat, Patricia

Paul, Paula, Pearly

Queen

Rachel

Raquel

Ray, Raynell,

Rickey, Richard, Ronita, Ronnie

Sharon

Shelia, Stefan, Susan

Tabitha, Tanya, Theresa, Tim

Uzoma

Valerie

Vernetta, Vicky

Wanda

Yolanda

Each friend is very special

Each friend is so unique

Just like every letter of the alphabet

Carrying nothing mystique.

12 Stones

I enjoy reading the Book of Joshua and reading about the 12 stones and what they represent. Once, I used the story of the 12 stones as a text for a mini-inspirational moment. It was a metaphoric story about my grandparents and their 10 children, thus creating the 12 Stones. The event is our annual Flood Family Reunion. We have had this family celebration every year since the family matriarch died in 1977. The original purpose was to celebrate the Flood Family legacy and memories of our fore parents. Well, it has gradually evolved and changed over the years into a full-size event. Initially, we used to sit around, laugh talk, and eat for several hours. We repeated this traditional format for many years with a new t-shirt of a different color. Some of us thought the reunion was too often and not enough activities for the younger generations at that time. The second generation, our parents, eventually turned it over to their children after many years. We, the third generation of first cousins, became the reunion coordinators. Each family had to designate a representative to attend the planning meeting and keep their family informed. New ideas and activities were created. A new t-shirt design was created with a different color every year. The event began to take on new meaning and follow a planned program with each family being represented in some way. For a few years, I had the privilege of writing and delivering short family inspirational messages. The one message that bonds with me the most was about the 12 Stones from the Book of Joshua chapter 4:1-9.

12 Stones

In the Biblical days
a long, long, long time ago
the Spirit of God dwelled
where the river of Jordan flowed.

The 12 tribes of Israel
traveled to the Promised Land
the land flowing with milk and honey
with the Ark of Covenant in hand.

They approached the Jordan
a river so deep and wide
They stopped at the shore and waited
for instructions to get to the other side.

God, the giver of life and breath
did not trade lives for loss
He held back the body of water
so every member could cross.

On dry ground they stepped
one man after the other
carrying the Ark of Covenant
each one regarded as a brother.

To the other side everyone made it
Praise and worship went up to God
who gave them grace and mercy
His abounding love did its part.

Lo, one member of each tribe
Commissioned to gather on his shoulder a stone
stack each one in a place
a place near the river and a place near home.

The 12 stones will serve a purpose
Each will serve among you as a sign
They are to be a memorial
of each tribal member's family ties.

"What do these stones mean?"
One day your children will ask
Tell them, "These stones are a memorial
for the people of Israel, forever." This is your life-long task.
Amen.

12 Family Stones

In the era of nineteen hundred and seventy-seven
about thirty something years ago
The first Flood Family Reunion began
as the generations began to grow

One, then two, three, four, five…ten children
Of Buddy and Ruth
Planned a family gathering
Based on love, fellowship, and truth

A reunion held at the family homestead
a placed called the Hill
at a quaint small house
no bigger than a box made for pills

Get ready, get ready
The Sunday of the Labor Day weekend
Come one, come all
Family and all ye friends

Each year brings the tradition
Family, food, t-shirts, and a familiar face
A brand new baby, a new generation
All coming together in this one place

The best of the reunion
Includes the food, activities, and fun
No strangers among us
Coming together all as one

Buddy and Ruth planted seeds
The original two stones
Planted deeply the family roots
and set the future generational tones

Today, there are four generations
With only 14 lives traded for loss
Built on prayer and a family legacy
and bent knees before the Cross

The ten children represent our family
A family of solid stones
Left in the place
The place Buddy and Ruth made home

They will serve as a purpose
Each will serve as a sign
And will be a memorial
Of your children's children family ties

"What do these stones mean?"
One day your children will ask
Tell them these 12 stones are a memorial
carrying on the Flood Family Reunion, forever. This is your task.

Chapter 5: Poetic Stories

from the Eyes of

Love

As an African American female, I am still searching for real love. I am truly inspired by the love I see among the President, his wife, and his family. To me, *The First Family* is the epitome of true unconditional love. This poem is inspired by the love I see looking in their world from the eyes of my windows.

The Love of a President

Real love is evident
in the face of our President
He loves his wife
he's forever grateful she is in his life.

Black love is radiating
precious love is illuminating
on their brown faces
in the White House and public places.

She shows her love in her smile
for her family she goes the extra mile
up close and personal she gets
and asking, "Dear, what's next?"

Family love is passed around
the same love is passed down
to the two little beautiful girls
who complete their world.

Unconditional love abides
deep within their humble pride
across America it is evident
the real love of a President.

Their love is not timid or shy
a love worth giving it a try
a strong handsome Black man
devoted to a loving Black woman.

A hug, a kiss, a warm embrace
up close, personal, in each other's face
The epitome of love prevails
in the love of the Obamas, Barack and Michelle.
April 25, 2010

All the best,

I was on medical leave at home recovering from cancer treatments. Every day at 2:00 p.m. for three months I would watch reruns of the *Steve Harvey Show*. I would schedule all of my treatments and appointments before or after the *Steve Harvey Show*. This was the one good thing that I looked forward to when I was down and out from the chemotherapy. My caregiver, friend, and cousin Barbara, came over every day to make sure I was comfortable. Barbara chuckled and said, *"You love Steve Harvey."* It was Barbara who told me that Steve Harvey was going to be at the Borders Bookstore in StoneCrest Mall in Lithonia, Georgia for his book signing. She showed it to me in the AJC; I cut it out and put it on my memo board. Then I pleaded with Barbara to drive me to the mall. Little did Steve Harvey know that I was a cancer patient, under chemotherapy, and losing my hair, yet I was standing in that line for his autograph. The mall was only 30 minutes away from my house. It was too close to forfeit this once in a life-time event. Barbara agreed. So, we bought our books and waited for that next Tuesday, 7:00 p.m. to arrive. We started out about 5:00 p.m. and headed to Stonecrest Mall. We thought we were early, but not so. The line had already started forming and wrapping itself through the corridor, and we were now in it. Thus, this is the story of *S.H. and a Flower.*

S.H. and a Flower

They say I am crazy about Steve Harvey
Yes, this is probably true
but not crazy-crazy in love
just admiration for him and his work too

I first fell for him
on the *Steve Harvey Show*
He played a good-looking teacher character
This you probably know.

Well, I heard he was coming to Stonecrest mall
He was signing autographs in his new book
I was home recovering from chemotherapy
but one word was all it took.

My cousin and caregiver at that time
arranged to drive me there
This was a special event
I had no time for worry or care.

We arrived at the mall
A long line we began to see
Oh well, we just had to stand in it
because it was Steve Harvey I wanted to see.

The long winding line inched up
minute by minute, hour by hour
Soon we would be close
and the turn would be ours.

We were getting closer,
and I saw him; I saw his head first
bald, shiny, and brown
one of his biggest fans was about to burst.

Of course, I was nervous
and anxious as a school girl
I was about to be near Steve Harvey
I was panicking out of this world.

I approached the table
The place where Steve sat
I handed him my book
but that wasn't just that.

"What's your name?" he asked
I told him in a clear and plain voice
"An-gel-li-a."
That's my name of course.

As he heard my name
his hand slipped across the page
"What just happened here?"
He asked aloud all amazed.

He signed his name, *Steve Harvey*
Then he added, "I'm going to give you a flower."
Lo, that was fine with me
because I had waited in that line for hours.

My time was up, and I had to move
and get out of the way
The line was still long
Others were still making their way.

Of course, I may not ever see him again
and he will never remember me
but I got an autograph and a flower
Look, here it is for you to see.

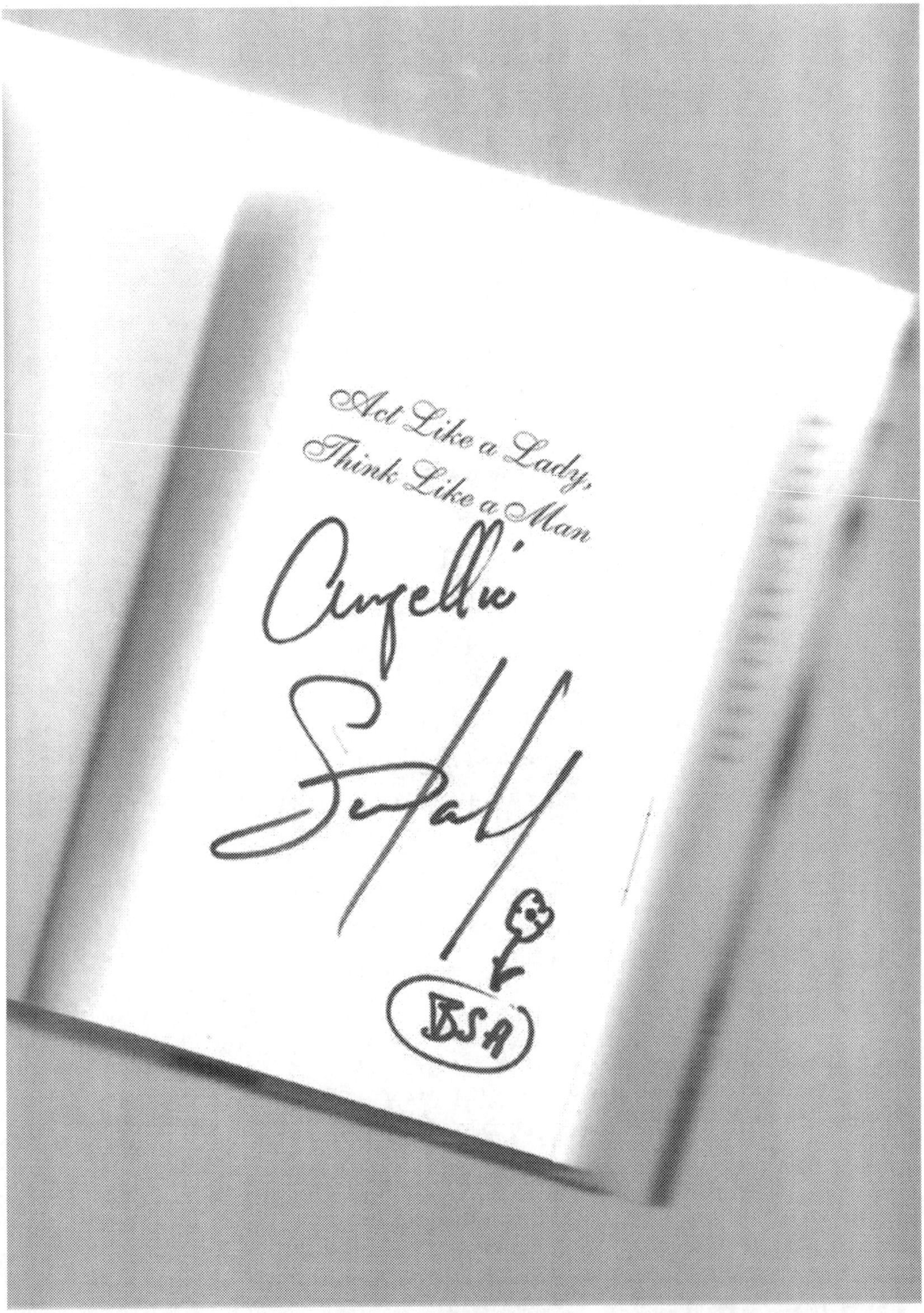
Act Like a Lady,
Think Like a Man

How do I love thee?

Let me count the ways.

I love thee to the depth and breadth and height my soul can reach

Elizabeth Barrett Browning

These are the lines from a poem that I remember reading, studying, and memorizing when I was a teenager. The lines rang true for me in 2002 when I met Mr. So and So. I think I fell head over heels in love with him. I would tease myself and say I would do whatever he said. If he said jump, I would jump and not even ask how high. If he said come here or go there, it was okay anything you say. If he only knew the power that he had over me, he could have used me to the maximum. I think I gave him some subtle hints on how much I wanted to love him and wanted us be the ideal couple. To this day, I do not know if he felt the same way, because he never expressed his feelings toward me. After three years of uncertain love, I decided to move on. I moved to Georgia. The only problem was I was still in love with him. Moving an extra 550 miles away from him did not change the fact that I was deeply in love. It is now 2010. I still think about him and wish that I could have been the one. Read this poetic love story. Read between the lines too.

Love Jones

It has been eight years now
that I first fell in love with you
I remember distinctly
it was February in the year 2002.

I saw you from afar
out of a window, I saw you pass by
you never saw me looking
but I saw you and gasped "Oh my!"

"Oh my, God!"
I silently said
a vision of loving you
plopped right in my head.

I remember that day
Oh so clear and oh so well
That was it; I was in
a Love Jones, under a love spell.

You wore a handsome blue suit
white shirt, dark shoes
I had to meet you,
what could I lose?

He came into the building
stepping into the hall
he was a little short
not that tall.

That was okay with me
I liked what my eyes saw
I was on a mission
to make a connection with this puzzling jigsaw.

His phone number I had to have
one step was all it took
His identity had to unfold
to me this guy was off the hook.

I made it a point
to get his digits
something I normally won't do
but, my mind was in circling orbits.

A long distance romance began
long distances, short visits, longing smiles
I was in love and
my love didn't care about the 400 miles.

Road trips and weekend visits
on the road to Maryland, again
to see the man I loved
I was his biggest fan.

He taught me to love him
and making love to him was sweet
it captured my mind
and dam! It swept me off my feet.

He taught me how to love
run hot, bubbly water in the tub
jump in with him
and give him a gentle massaging back rub.

Turn down the lights
and light one, two, or three candles
get the fragrance going
and hold him by his love handles.

Close your eyes let your thoughts go
let your imagination kick in
relax and let love
take over and do it again.

I wanted this to be forever
I wanted to be his wife
but for some reason he just wasn't
having me full time in his life.

I thought, let's live together
let me move there
I just want to be with you
hell! I don't care.

One time I remember
writing him a love letter
I put that message in a bottle
I was deeply in love and didn't know any better.

Today, I can hardly remember
a word of what I said
it was my thoughts about him and
the thoughts in my heart and head.

I never found out what he thought
he read it but didn't respond
did I win, did I lose?
His heart had I won?

Soon my loved turned south
and I began to feel sad it seemed
serious disappointment abound
maybe he wasn't the man of my dream.

I desperately wanted us to be a couple
I was his; if only he were mine
I wished we could be together
day, night, and all the time.

He was not good about phone calls
and he seldom called me
I wanted to talk with him often
Couldn't he see?

My eyes grew sad
my soul became depressed
why couldn't he just love me
without me feeling stressed?

I even talked about me
moving there, with him in his house
Let's move in together
hinting that I wanted to be his spouse.

Nothing happened
no confirmation came out of his mouth
so, I packed up my things
and I moved to Georgia...further south.

I cried and I prayed
the pain was a deep inner sting
I just could not get over
this Love Jones thing.

One year, two years
three years went by
I still remember seeing him
and saying Oh my!

It's been eight years now
since the day we first met
I'm not as much in love
but my memory is deeply set.

I guess I should get over it
I guess I should say goodbye
Guess what, I still pray to God
and I still wish, that he were the guy.

I shall wait on God
and I shall be free
this Love Jones
has to let go of me.

This poetic story has three titles. I did not know which title to give this poem; Two guys Named Harold, Harold to the 2nd Power, or Hrld^2. Anyway, it is about two distinctly different guys at different periods of time in my life. It's ironic because many of the guys I know have the same name. I know two guys with the name Jeffrey of Jeff. I know two guys with the name Derek. A few of those names are spelled differently, for example, Deric and Derek. I know two guys with the name Harold. Harold is spelled only one way. This is what I have to say about the two guys with the same name Harold.

Two Guys Named Harold

Once in 1983
I met this handsome guy you see
He was tall, thin
Made just right
His name was Harold
And he was White.

I worked in a department store
as a receptionist part time.
He worked there too
Only he worked full time.
I worked at the main desk
He was middle management
Sharp and at his best.

We talked a little and
He often stopped by
Realizing a little attraction
We caught each other's eye.
Cool, I thought
Enjoying his attention

Making it clear, I was interested
Just thought I'd mention.

I mustered the courage
To ask if he'd consider a dinner date
"Sure", he said
And did not hesitate.
Harold, white and sexy
Honest and sincere
Visions of being with him
Rang in my imagination, so clear.

Kiss him, caress him
That's what I would do
Climb on top of his white body
Get it on, just us two.

We never did go out
We never finished the date
I soon left the company
I guess it was then too late.
Life moved on
This rendezvous came to an end
To this day
I have never seen Harold again.

Ten years later in 1993
I met this handsome guy you see
He was tall, thin
Made just right
His name was Harold
But he wasn't white.

I worked in the public school
As an elementary teacher
He worked on the sea as a sailor
Oh, and I also became a church leader.
I saw him here and there
He saw me around too
one sharp and good-looking dude
ordinary and cool.

We talked a lot and
He often called me late at night
Talking sweet nothings
much fun and pure delight.
Cool, I thought
Enjoying his attention
Making it clear, I was interested
Just thought I'd mention.

I mustered the courage
To ask if he'd consider a dinner date
"Sure", he said
and did not hesitate.
Harold, hot and so fine
Elusive and aloof
Kept me second guessing
I couldn't get a serious break through.

He got married
But not to me
Shocked me like hell
I was stunned as can be.

We never did go out
We never finished our date
He stood me up
And that was our fate.
Life moved on
I put this rendezvous to an end
I told this Harold to get out of my life
Cause I never want to see him again.

By no means am I a Hip Hop music fan. However, I am a people fan. The men and women who sing/rap Hip Hop music are very creative. I believe they are people too, and they deserve respect as musical artists and geniuses. Many of these artists are hard-working, doing what's right, and making an honest living. One of my favorite artists is the one and only Ludacris or Luda for short. Guest what. I don't know anything about his music, not one song. In this case, it is not about his music. It is about the person bringing the music.

For You, Luda!

Ludacris is one of my favorite rappers
not because he raps so well
but it's his character, demeanor
That makes him swell.

He is a handsome young man
cool, articulate, intelligent
Treats women with respect
He must be a real gent.

Ladies, ladies, ladies
Ludacris is the man
Catch his eye
Catch him if you can!

Luda has a smooth face
sugar-glazed pecan brown
He is fine
and gets my vote, hands down!

Angellia Moore

Well kept, neat, with the look
Thin and built so fine
Made just right
Might blow your mind.

A deep heavy and
sexy voice
would, could, should be every woman's
man of choice.

He is one with talent
A hip hop bro
A rapping artist
for sho'.

Rapping and dapping
and bringing it on so fast
Watch out, watch out
Luda might kick yo' @$$

Ludacris better known as Luda
Makes all the ladies scream
This one's for you, Luda
You're a good man, at least it seems.

It seems that love and suicide just go together. It was part of Romeo and Juliet's love story. It is often part of today's love stories as well. I met Tony through his sister Linda, unplanned. She and I worked part time in a local department store at the mall. One day, I was visiting her at her apartment. Just so happened on that same day her brother decided to pay her a visit. She introduced us. He saw me and liked what he saw, and I saw him and liked what I saw. So, we were instantly attracted to each other.

I was a college graduate just starting out on my own. He was a local laborer, older guy, father, so what, everybody needs somebody to love. Well, from that day, we began our Romeo and Juliet love story. Our romance lasted for about two years. That's the love part now let me tell you the whole story.

Love and Suicide

He and I liked each other right away
We began seeing each other day after day

I was young, right out of college
He was a laborer, with looks and basic knowledge

He regularly came over to my place
We were lovey-dovey in each other's face

We did things together, here and there
I thought we were a good solid pair

It wasn't long before he moved in
okay… cohabitating, shacking up, living in sin

This is where I found out more about his life
Hiding a cocaine drug habit each night

I never saw him snort,
and I let that be my blind recourse

Although I did ask him to give it up,
but it was too hard for him, too abrupt

I was in love, so it didn't matter
Little did I know our lives would soon be shattered

Time passed and I thought we should get married
He said, "I've already done the baby and carriage."

What? What does that have to do with me?
I am not her! Can't you see?

He told me that he'd been married before
Let's just be in love and ignore and explore

I wasn't having it—no way
Another turning point came that day

In spite being faced with these things
I did not want to leave, but trouble it would bring

That summer, I went home to stay with my family
They had no idea of the hidden calamity

Of course, he did not want that,
but I had to put him in check

He called me and pleaded his case
Please come back without haste

At first I thought, *sure, let's try again,*
but something changed my mind from within

I relocated to another place and time
That's when he took his own life and some of mine

I never imagined suicide would be his fate
He put a gun to his head then it was too late

The police chaplain knocked on my door
He said, "We were concerned for you, Ms. Moore

Your name and letters were in his place
Just wanted to let you know face to face

Your x-boyfriend is now dead
From a single self-inflicted gunshot wound to his head

I was hit with a biting and a stinging pain
Deep in my body, deep in my veins

Grief was nailed all over me
A pain that you could almost see

I went into a spaced-out daze
Stayed there for weeks, months, years…just in a haze

For ten years that pain lingered
Memories, guilt, flashbacks, all kinds of stingers

Every day was like yesterday
Love and suicide surely don't play.

I hate to be wasteful, throwing away perfectly good love. Surely, we all have wasted good love at one time or another trying to put it in the wrong place at the wrong time. It's unfortunate that the human race has such a hard time of establishing and maintaining relationships. If only we could love God's way and get this love thing right, then we won't have *Wasted Love*.

Wasted Love

Wasted love
gone
down the drain
phone calls
seldom returned
dry kisses
void of sweetness
cold caresses
void of tenderness
sexless nights
love
gone sour
stone cold
exasperated
no more visits
no one is home
swollen eyes
filled with tears
hurting heart
confused mind
figuring you out

Angellia Moore

frustrated
never a solid merger
bare ring finger
no diamond ring
no glitter
no gold
wasted years
gone
down the drain
wasted love.

My favorite American-made car is the Chevy Camaro. It is a classic sports car, and it has the looks that change over time. But it remains on the classic car list. It remains on my list as my favorite car.

My Chevy Camaro

About a decade ago, I bought a Chevy
It was cute as can be
A sporty T-Top Camaro
Sleek, cool and waiting for me.

The day I first saw it
I bypassed it on the spot,
but I looked at it over my shoulder
I looked back like Lot.

I knew it was the car
Silver and shiny on the outside
Soft, gray comfortable
Low and just right on the inside.

I made my selection
A T-top convertible with five speeds
Speeding down the highway
Seeking and fulfilling my needs.

Oh yeah, it was recognizable
VQH460 was its ID
People saw it coming
and knew it was me.

Once I was speeding on Highway 58
Going 73 in a 55 zone
The police on the opposite side
put his blue lights on.

I pulled over and waited on the side of the road
I knew those blue lights were for me
I knew I was getting a ticket
Like I said, I just waited there patiently.

"Slow down, Ms. Moore
and have a nice day"
"Yes sir," I said
and the officer was on his way.

One ticket, two tickets, three
a few fender benders or two
poor Chevy Camaro
was damaged and no longer shiny and new.

Regardless, I kept my Chevy Camaro
She was mine for six more years
Wheeling, dealing, speeding
and shifting those manual five gears.

I loved my Chevy Camaro
I love it still to this day
I miss it very much
but as fate would have it, I traded it away.

A very popular female Rhythm and Blues (R & B) artist once sang a song with the lyrics "I'm searching for a *Real Love*; someone to set my heart free". I guess you could say that I am searching for that real love too. Well, maybe I am not searching. I am just remaining hopeful. In the meantime, I will just write down all of the characteristics that I want this particular love to have. Sometimes, I feel that God did not create anyone for me whose ribs fit mine. Just in case He did, this poem is called *Wanted*.

Wanted

Wanted, S.A.M
Single Attractive Man
free to live and love
destined to fine his half
any way he can

Wanted, S.A.M
five feet nine almost six
up to 180 pounds, built
not a body on sticks.

Wanted, S.U.M
Single Urban Man
well-groomed, fine
blue or black suit, shiny shoes
barber-shop kind.

Wanted, S.U.M
strong in living his life
priorities in order
able to conquer
stresses and strife.

Wanted, S.U.M
Owner of a hot BMW
sports car, classic car, or luxury ride
Can start as friends
until we get in stride.

Wanted, S.B.M
Single Black Man
of high intellect
takes advantage of education
talented, brings in that pay check.

Wanted, S.B.M
Selfless, noble
Giving of all his love
Wrapped in a smooth package
pecan-brown from God above.

I was a little girl of about six or seven years of age when my family discovered I had a mass or a lump on the right side of my neck. That lump was about the size of a quarter. It seemed to move a little here and there to the touch. It's rather vague to me now, but I remember my mother and another family being very fussy about that lump on my neck. I never had treatment for it. I never had surgery. I never took any medicine for it. It just up and went away.

However, today, I may have a predisposition to lumps and masses because every now and then, another mass is found in my body. I have had surgery to remove fibroids, cysts, and auxiliary masses here and there. Anyway, the most important thing is that they were all benign growths. The most recent lump found didn't go away so easily. It turned out to be cancerous. It grew fast and reached stage three metastasis. It required immediate action.

Nothing but Love: My Cancer Story

Summer, July, in the year 2008
I was exercising at home
using a pair of five-pound hand weights.

Reach 2- 3- 4- 5- 6- 7- 8
Stretch 2- 3- 4- 5- 6- 7- 8
Push 2- 3- 4- 5- 6- 7- 8
Stretch 2- 3- 4- 5- 6- 7- 8

Working out the best I could
Simple exercises you know
On a regular basis like I should.

In the middle of a full right reach
I felt a tightening pull in my breast
I stopped instantly to check each.

The left breast was fine,
but not the right one
there was a mass the size of a dime.

I thought to myself, oh no.
Can this really be a mass
another one you know?

I would take a Mammogram in about a week
Surely, I would mention it
to the physician as we speak.

Yes, there was cause for concern
cancer is on the rise
more information we all have to learn.

To check the malignancy of the cells
A biopsy was next in order
From this, much they could tell.

I wished the results were negative
but, the cells were cancerous
The results came back positive.

A waiting lady saw my tears
On the spot she prayed for me
and asked God to wipe away my fears.

Thank you for your spiritual love.

The doctor and his team advised
Please, don't wait on this, Ms. Moore
Waiting could be your demise.

Decisions were of the urgency
I had to think fast,
This was by far, my greatest emergency.

Those malignant cells could spread fast
Delays in addressing cancer
Means one could quickly past.

Surgery I agreed to go through
To remove the growing mass
and all of the breast tissues too.

The date was the 23 of December
Surgery was scheduled for me
That date I will always remember.

I did what I had to do
I called my family
and gave them the grave news too.

They immediately mapped out a plan
"We have to go to Georgia", Jackie said
"all who can."

This was a few days before the Christmas holiday
The family had to revise
the entire celebration for that day.

They packed every SUV they had
It was so special,
with food, presents, and people, I was glad.

My surgery went well
I recovered that night in the hospital
No more cancer cells that they could tell.

I felt very little discomfort and pain
Although this was a major surgery
Cool, calm, and collected I remain.

I must commend the medical team
The surgeon was excellent
and the nurses were a dream.

Thank you for your love and service.

I arrived home on December twenty-fourth
My house had been transformed
A Christmas wonderland brought forth.

Seventeen family members were in my house
My mother, nieces, and nephews
sisters, brothers, and somebody's spouse.

They celebrated Christmas as they usually do
I felt very little discomfort
So, I celebrated Christmas too.

Thank you for a family's love.

After Christmas, the family was gone
Jackie stayed back to help me
She didn't want to leave me alone.

Jackie cooked, cleaned, and prayed
Totally cared for me
I was glad she stayed.

We collected and placed scriptures everywhere
They were all over the house
To this day, they are still there.

After two weeks, she had to leave
I was okay by then
For in God I trusted and believed.

My sister, Cass, her Persnickety behaviors like a mother hen
spent two weeks with me
checking on me, her family, and her friends.

My brother, Kenny was handy with his tools
He was covertly concerned about the cancer
He just wanted to make everything cool.
Thank you for sisterly and brotherly love.

Barbara stuck by my side
She sat with me day in and day out
She never let my spirit take a dive.

Barbara encouraged me along the way
Her faith held us together
and kept us going day by day.

Thank you for a caregiver's love.

One never knows how much people care
Until you go through something
then their love shows up right there.

Many people showed their thoughtfulness
the multitude of cards, letters, emails, and gifts
A massive outpouring of genuine kindness.

I received over a 100 get-well cards
Each one with a special message
Straight from their hearts.

The many phone calls came in too
I did not mind
Certainly, I needed to hear from each of you.

My friends and coworkers visited to wish me well
Bearing things that I needed
water, fruit, magazines, books, and more mail.

Thank you for unconditional love.

One niece, Deet, wept and cried
We had to console her
and help to dry her weeping eyes.

Travis was stunned beyond words to say
"Free yourself, be yourself." I said
"I will be okay."

Darryl G. called me all the time
Not much on conversation
Just checking to see if I was doing fine.

Thank you for a precious love.

My uncle and his wife drove many miles
crossing several state lines
bringing well wishes and sweet smiles.

My aunt, Catherine came with a car load too
Darlene and Marvin, Trisha, Carol,
and a granddaughter, to name a few.

Thank you for a family's love.

Once I saw my mother cry
She was engulfed with fears of death
I knew that was the reason why.

Thank you for a mother's love.

Even me, I had a hard moment
"Run on, see what the end will be."
God said, and away those doubts went.

Me, with a serious disease
Cancer, I never saw it coming
Just unreal, too hard to believe.

God wiped away everybody's surprise
He got everybody straight
Providing comfort for crying eyes.

Thank you for a Father's love.

Today, I am cancer free
two years after that faithful day of discovery
I can still praise God and worship Thee.

These are the Biblical scriptures that set me free from worry and anxiety as I went through the cancer and chemotherapy.

Matthew 17:20 If you have faith as a mustard seed, you will say to this mountain, "move from here to there", and it will move, and will be impossible for you.

Proverbs 3:5-6 Trust in the Lord with all thine heart, lean not unto thy own understanding. In all thy ways acknowledge Him, and He shall direct thy paths.

Psalm 139:4 I will praise you, for I am fearfully and wonderfully made.

1 Timothy 6:12 Fight the good fight of faith, lay hold on eternal life, to which you were also called and have confessed the good confession.

Mark 9:23 Jesus said to him, "If you can believe all things are possible to him who believes."

2 Corinthians 5:7 For we walk by faith, not by sight.

Isaiah 53:5 But he was wounded for our transgressions; he was bruised for our iniquities; the chastisement for our peace was upon him, and by his stripes we are healed.

Jeremiah 29:11 I know the thoughts I think toward you, says the Lord, thoughts of peace and not of evil, to give you a future and a hope. Then you will call upon me and pray to me, and I will listen to you.

Psalm 16:8-9 I have set the Lord always before me; because he is at my right hand, I shall not be moved.

Psalm 100: 2 Serve the Lord with gladness; come before his presence with singing.

Psalm 27:14 Wait on the Lord, be of good courage and he shall strengthen thine heart; wait I say on the Lord.

Psalm 37:4 Delight thyself also in the Lord. Trust also in him, and he shall bring it to pass.

Hebrew 11:1 Now, faith is the substance of things hoped for, the evidence of things not seen.

Matthew 9:18-22 Be of good cheer daughter, your faith has made you well.

Taking the chemotherapy treatments remind me of the bitter but sweetness of childbirth. Childbirth is quite painful at the time that you are in it, however, shortly after the pain subsides the anxiety goes away and joy comes. So it is with chemotherapy treatments. It will make you sick as can be while going through, but as the chemo passes through your body, you begin to feel better and temporarily forget the nausea, vomiting, and sickness until next the next treatment.

Chemotherapy: That's Another Story

The time had come, January 2009
taking chemotherapy was fresh on my mind

I heard vicious rumors about it
That you definitely will get sick.

Six treatments I had to take
Each one holding my destiny at stake.

Three sacks of clear chemical medicine
Slowly dripping from needles under my skin.

Nausea began to give my stomach an ache
Making my nerves quiver and quake.

Slowly sifting, stripping me of energy
fatigue physically taking over me.

One treatment and I just about died
Vomiting, gagging, tears in my eyes.

I shall take this medicine no more
As I lay crumpled on the floor.
Five more treatments… this medicine again!
Surely, this chemical will do me in.

After three days the sickness passed
but my belly still had chemical gas.

For those few days I could not eat
I could barely stand on my feet.

Four more treatments I had to endure
more chemical treatment for sure.

At the mere thought of it
caused my mouth to water and make me sick.

I had to keep a positive outlook
Counting down each treatment was all it took.

They were dwindling and going fast
I was down to three treatments at last.

My body grew gaunt, narrow, and thin
So did my face, cheeks, and chin.

Another side effect was loss of my hair
At first, it was too hard to bear.

Then, I began to wear a cranial prosthesis or wig
Red, poufy, long, and big.

By now I was learning to cope
but the chemical still made me gag and choke.

Two final treatments to take
I can do this for heaven sake.

Three or four days in then out
Afterwards, for joy I could really shout.

Oh, my happiest day
was that final treatment in May.

Now, I was well and doing great
Chemical therapy I love but hate.

Treatments did what they were designed to do
Make me well and restore my cells to new.

The cancer is in what is called remission
I can live on now with God's unspoken permission.

God's Holy Spirit helped me write this work. It was important to me to write from inspired thoughts, actual events, real people, and real issues. These poetic stories are captured from the eyes of my windows or from my perspective, which means, this is the way I see things. It contains stories from snapshots of actual events that I once lived. Now, just because I see things from the eyes of my window as I do, does not make it so. These poetic stories are not written with any malicious intent, hatred, contempt, disgust, or dislikes, only from the eyes of windows.

REFERENCE NOTES

Barcenas, Y. (2008), Poem to Ms. Moore

Blige, M. J. (1992) Real Love, Uptown Records

Cesar, S. No Charge

Harvey, S. (2009), Act Like a Lady, Think Like a Man

Penney, J.C. (2010)

The Holy Bible (1990), King James Version

The White House, Obama Family Portrait

White, R. N., (2010), Animation Artist – From the Eyes of My Windows